Color My Flaws

Body Positive Adult Coloring Book
By
Isaac Snagg

Color My Flaws! In this book you see illustrations of real people and what they had to say about their bodies, what they see in the mirror, and how they feel about who they see. I wanted to make something positive about the things we all have learned to see as "flaws". From stretch marks to love handles to penis size, we all have felt insecure at one moment or another in our lives. With the Color My Flaws adult coloring book I hope to allow people to take a deeper look at each "flaw" and see that this is your body and there is nothing to be ashamed of! Color it in however you'd like. It's already your masterpiece.

Thanks to the women and men who posed for this

Special Thanks To Rebecca a.k.a "Love"

My Reason

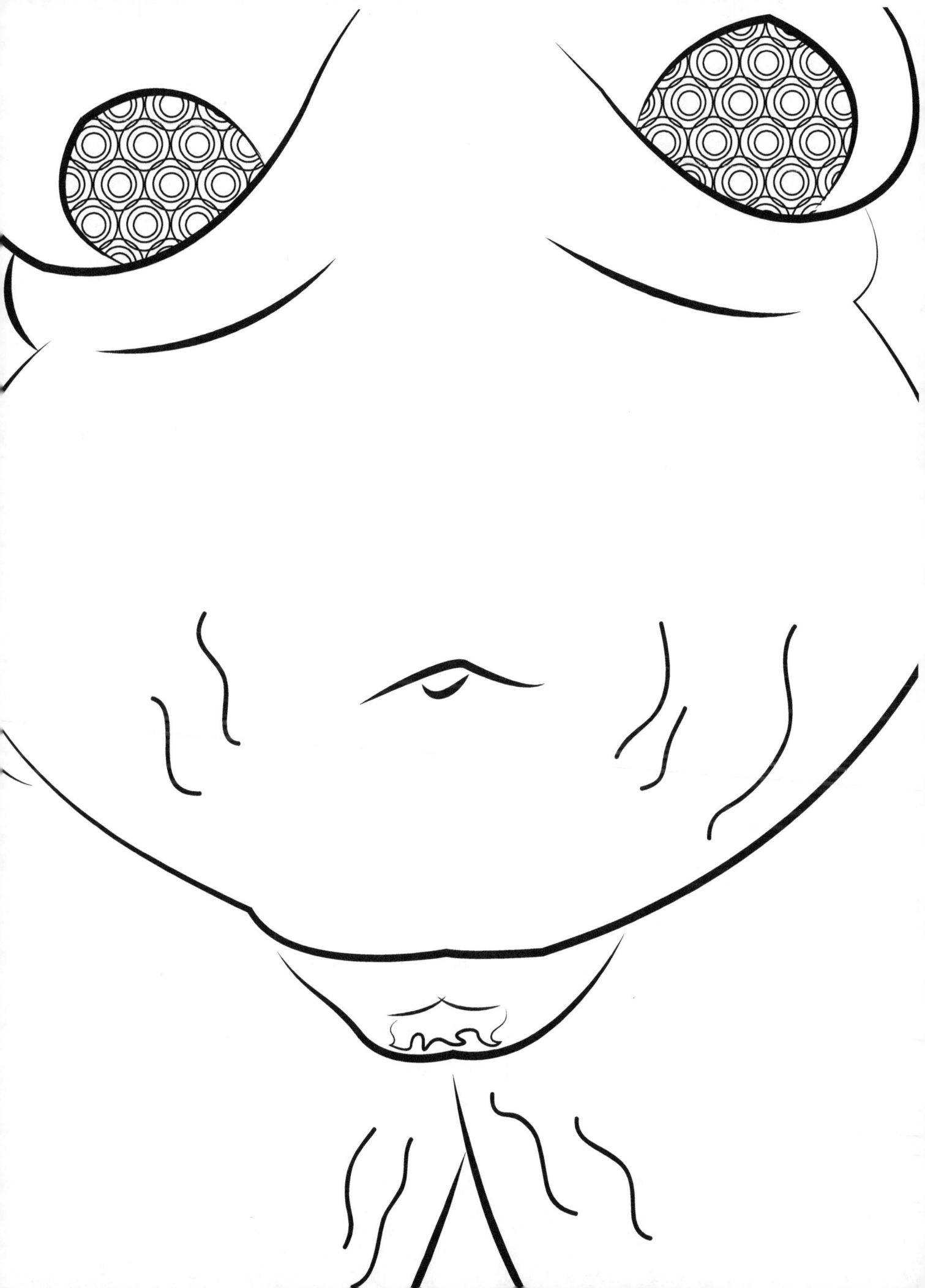

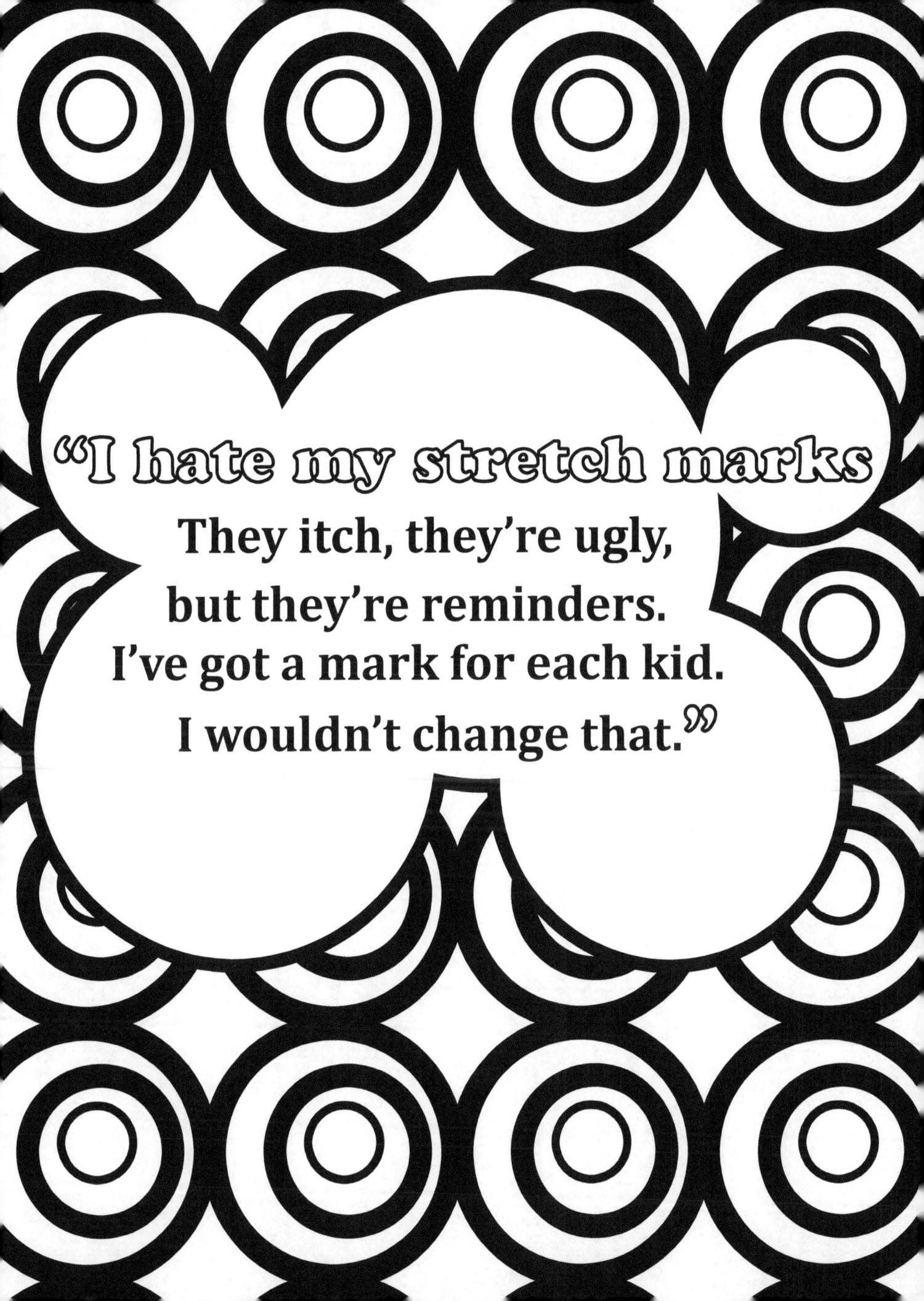

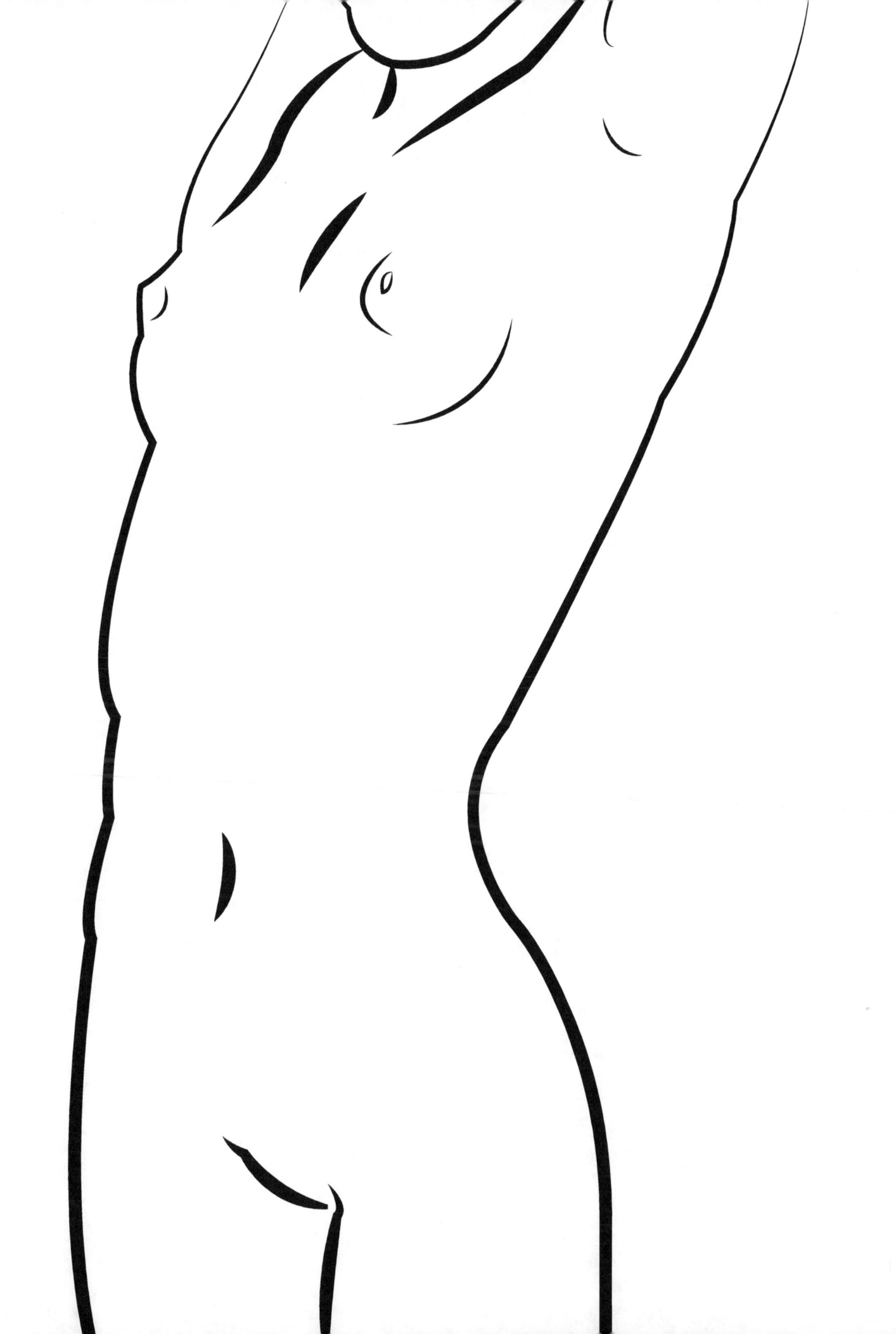

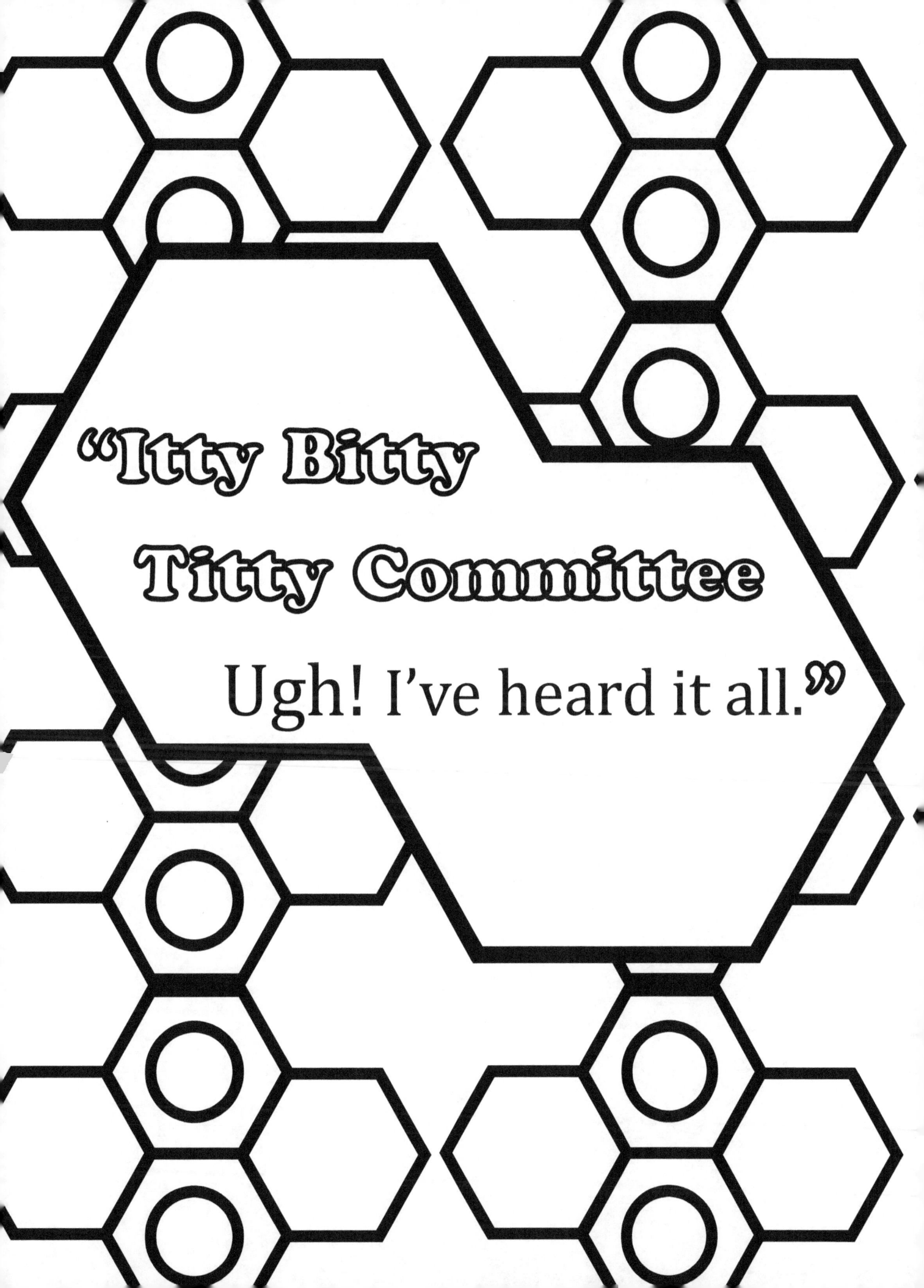

"Itty Bitty Titty Committee

Ugh! I've heard it all."

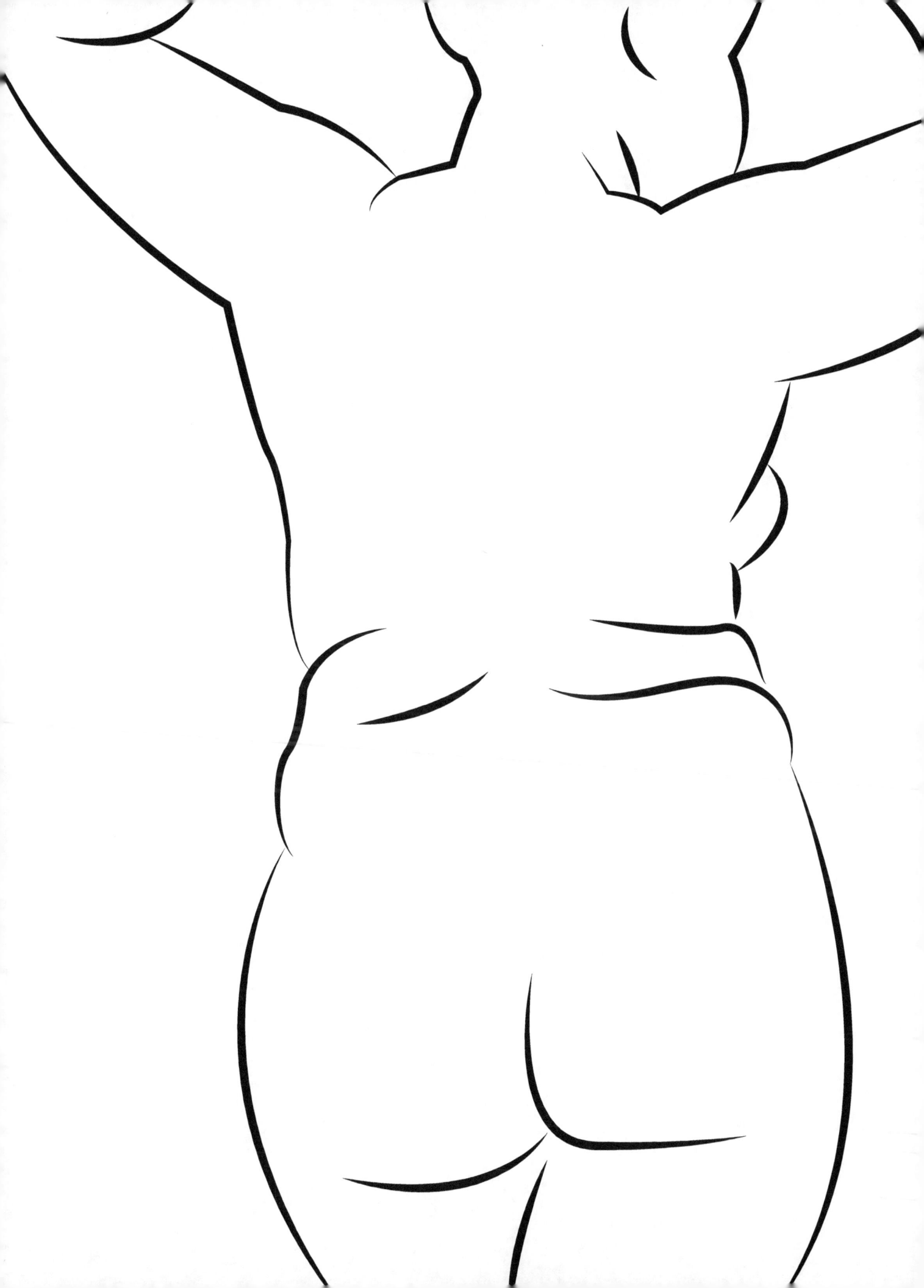

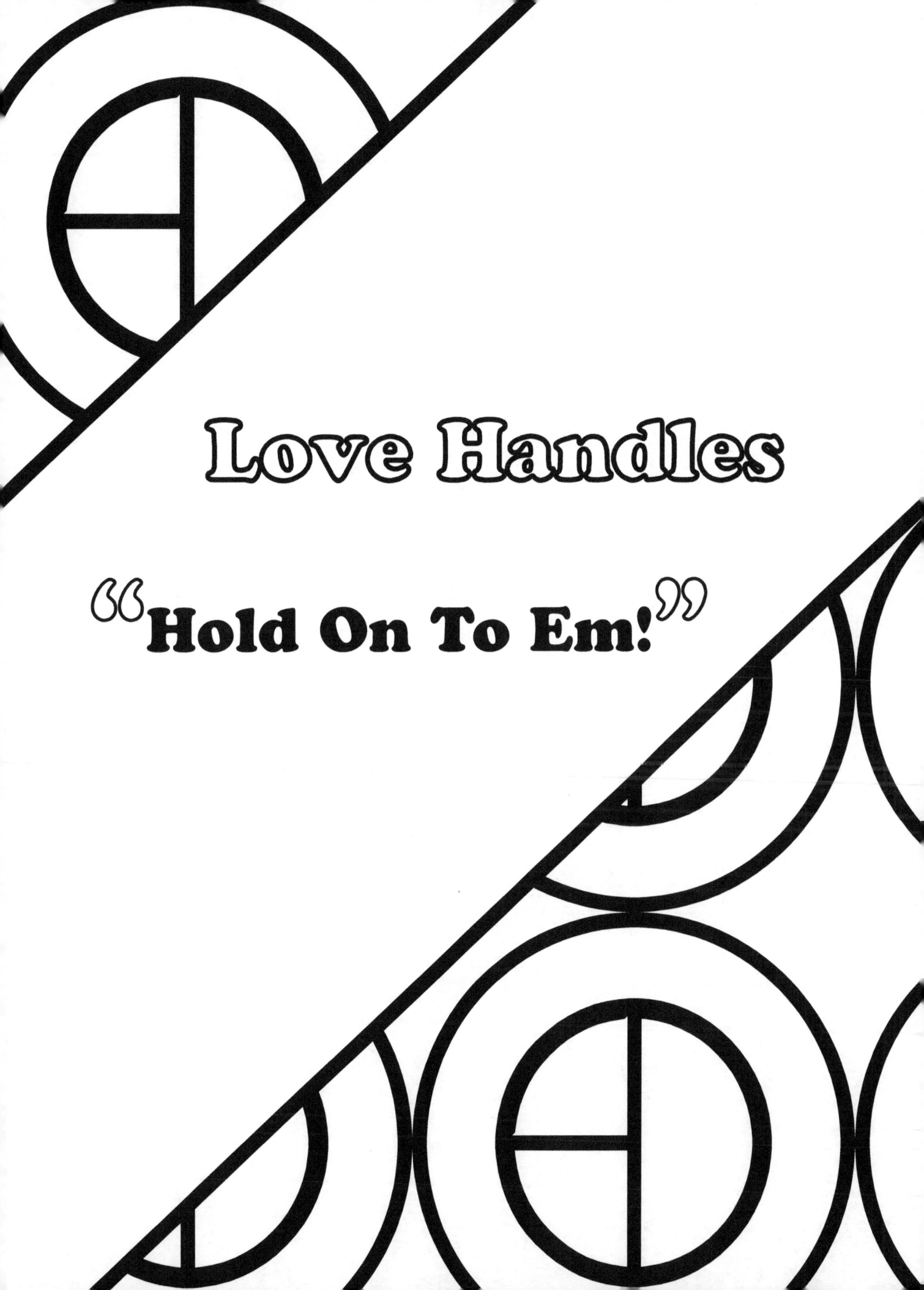

Love Handles

"Hold On To Em!"

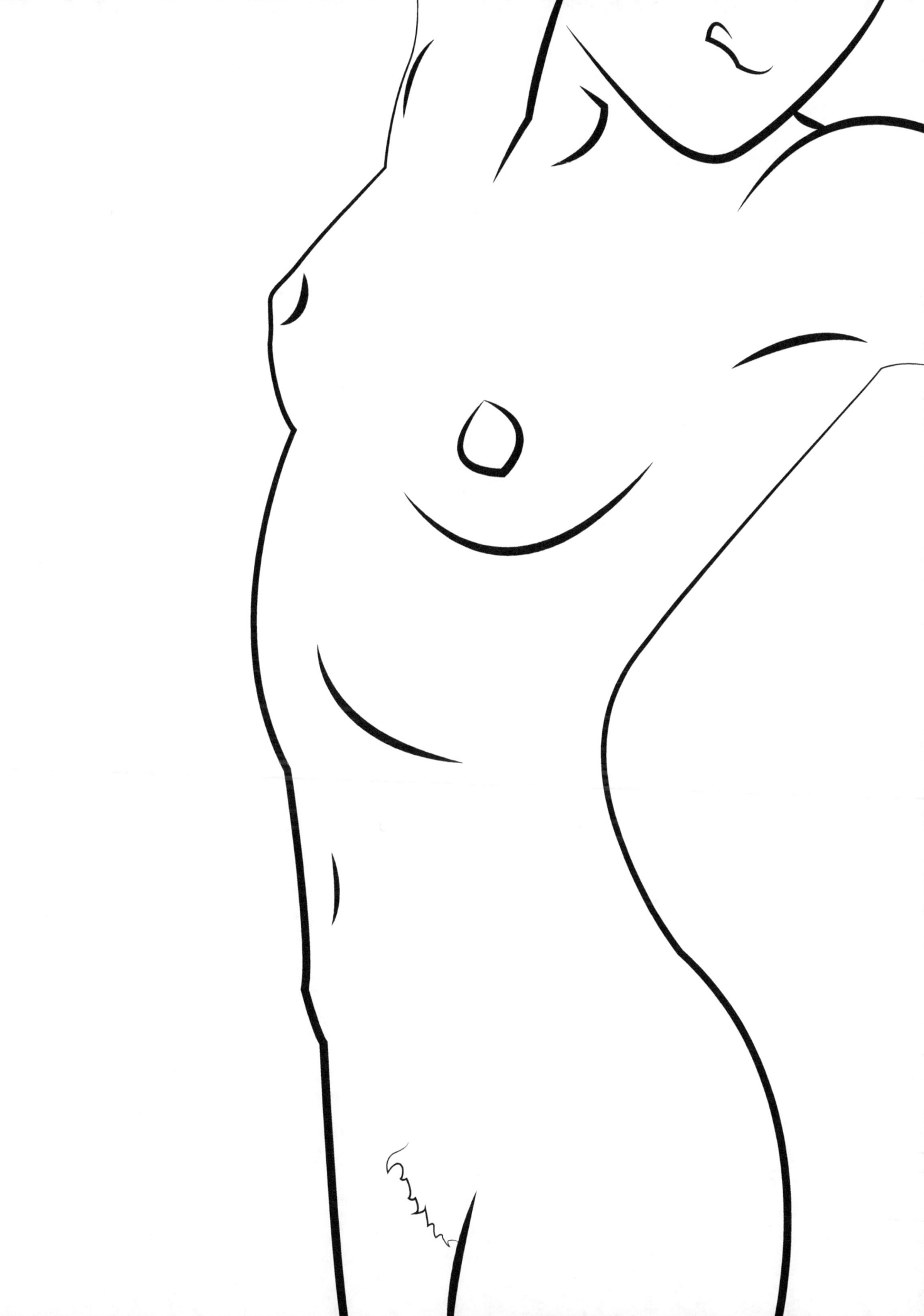

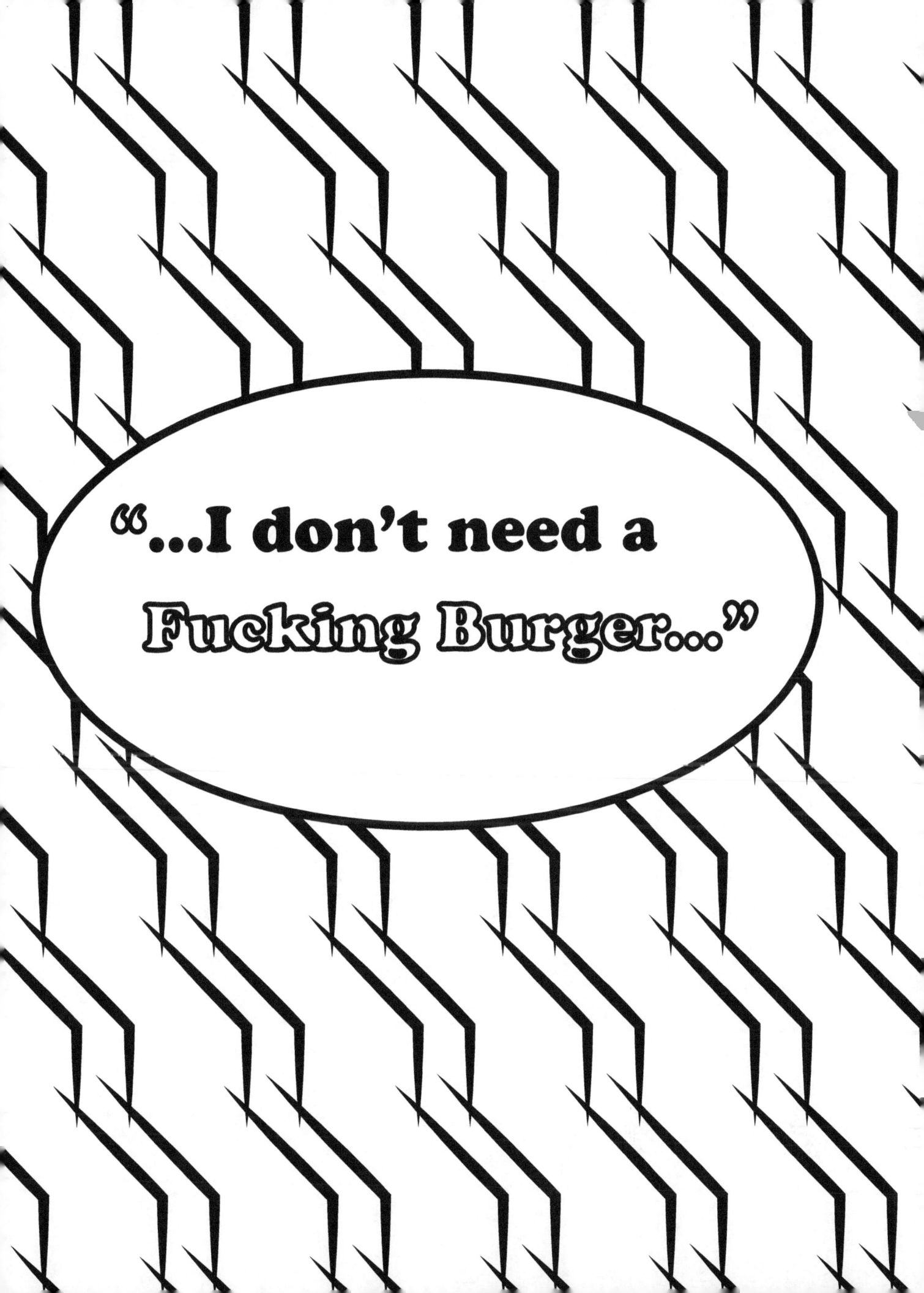

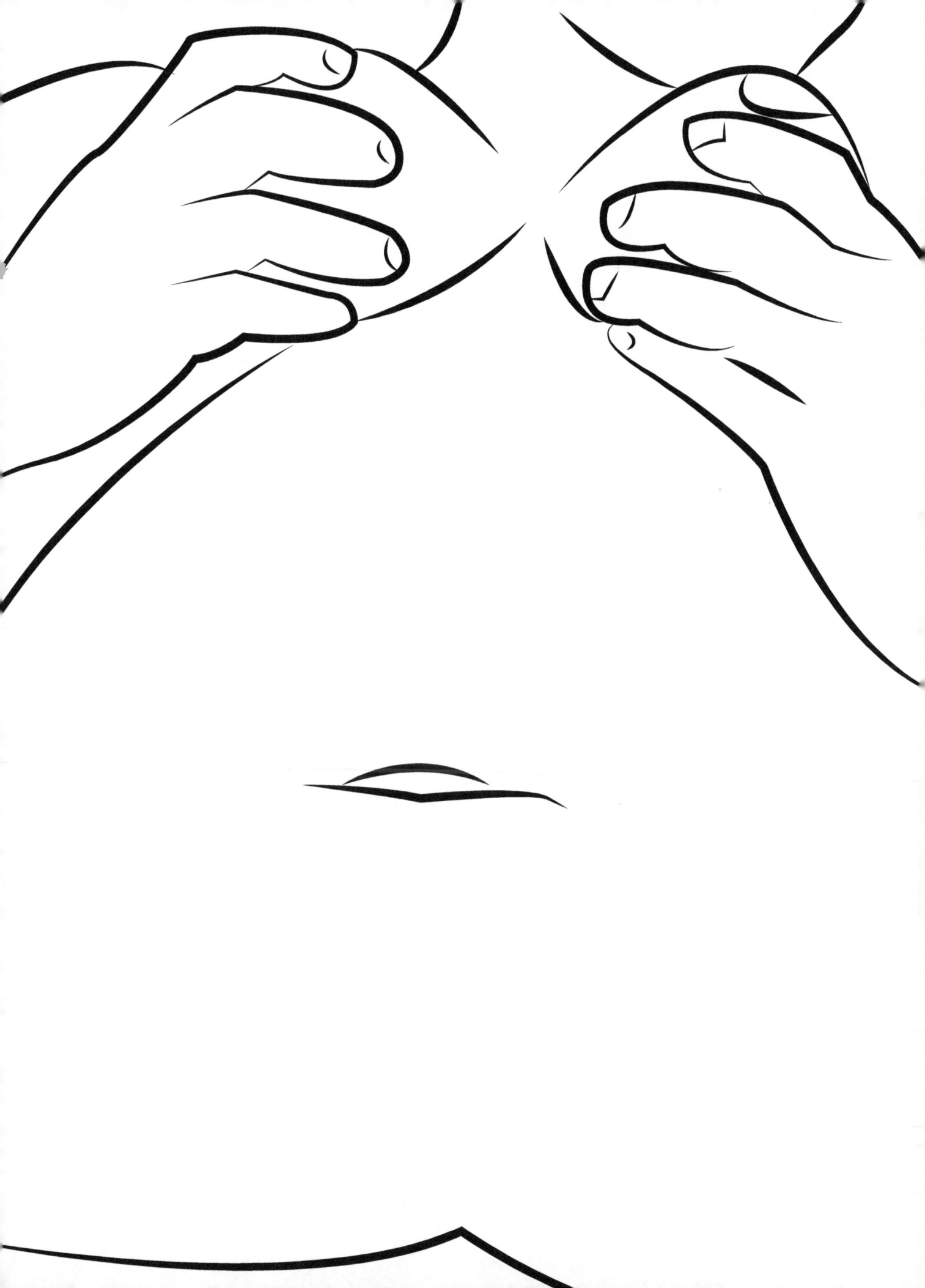

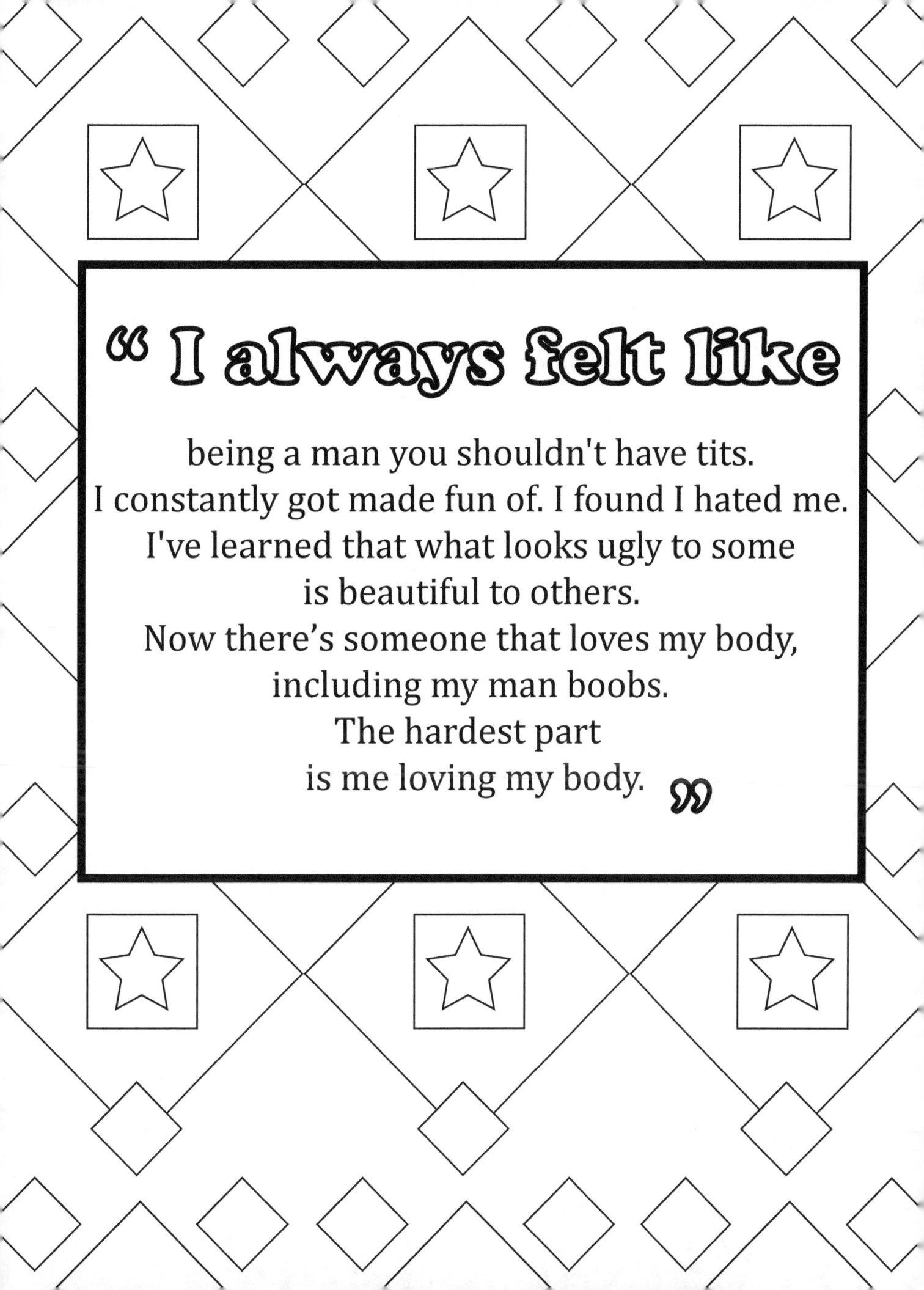

" I always felt like

being a man you shouldn't have tits.
I constantly got made fun of. I found I hated me.
I've learned that what looks ugly to some
is beautiful to others.
Now there's someone that loves my body,
including my man boobs.
The hardest part
is me loving my body. "

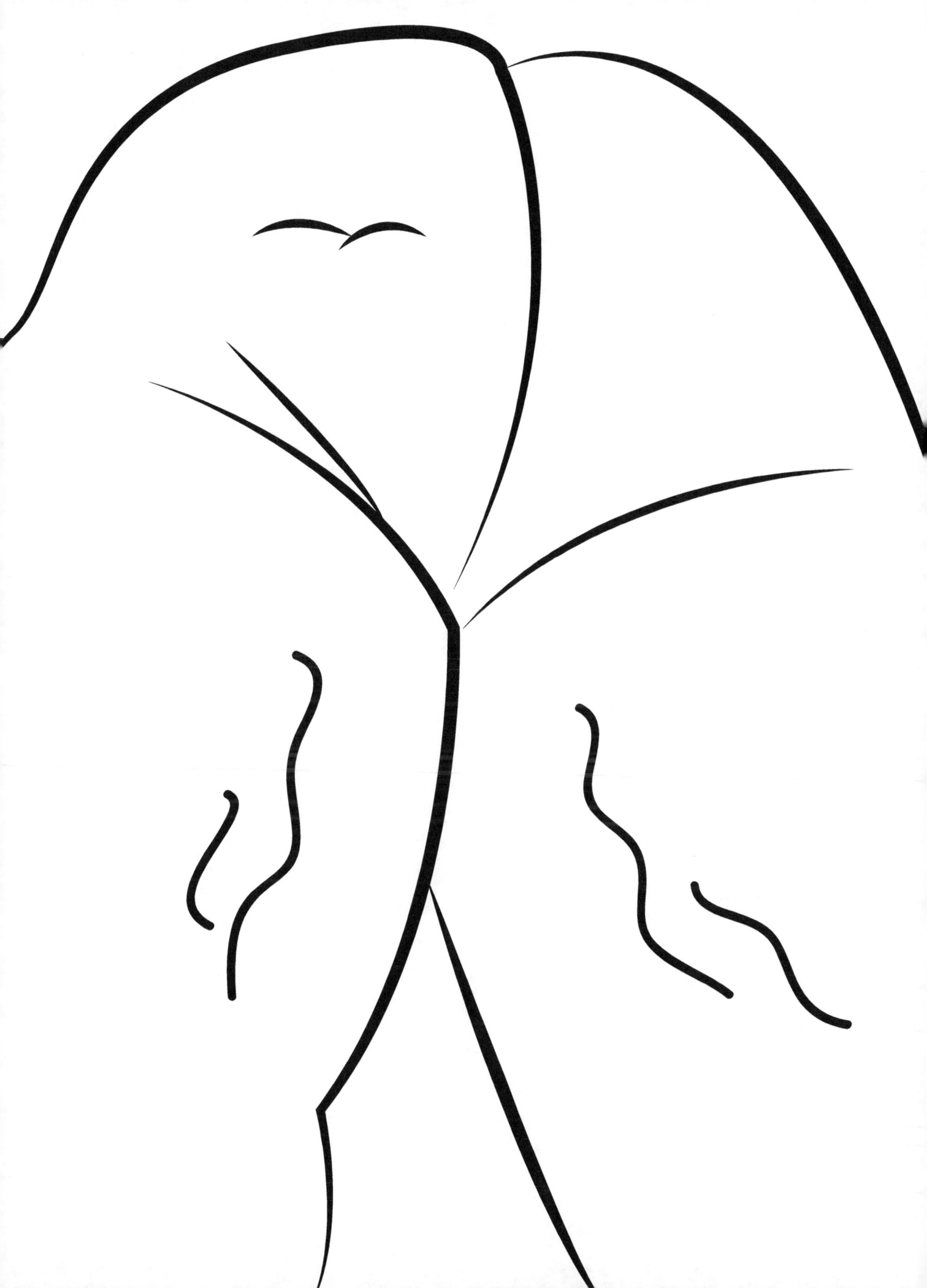

" Cottage Cheese, Butt Dimples

I know all the names for it.
You name it, I've heard em.
I got a phat ass, a dunk,
I'm bootylicious
I know all the good names too. "

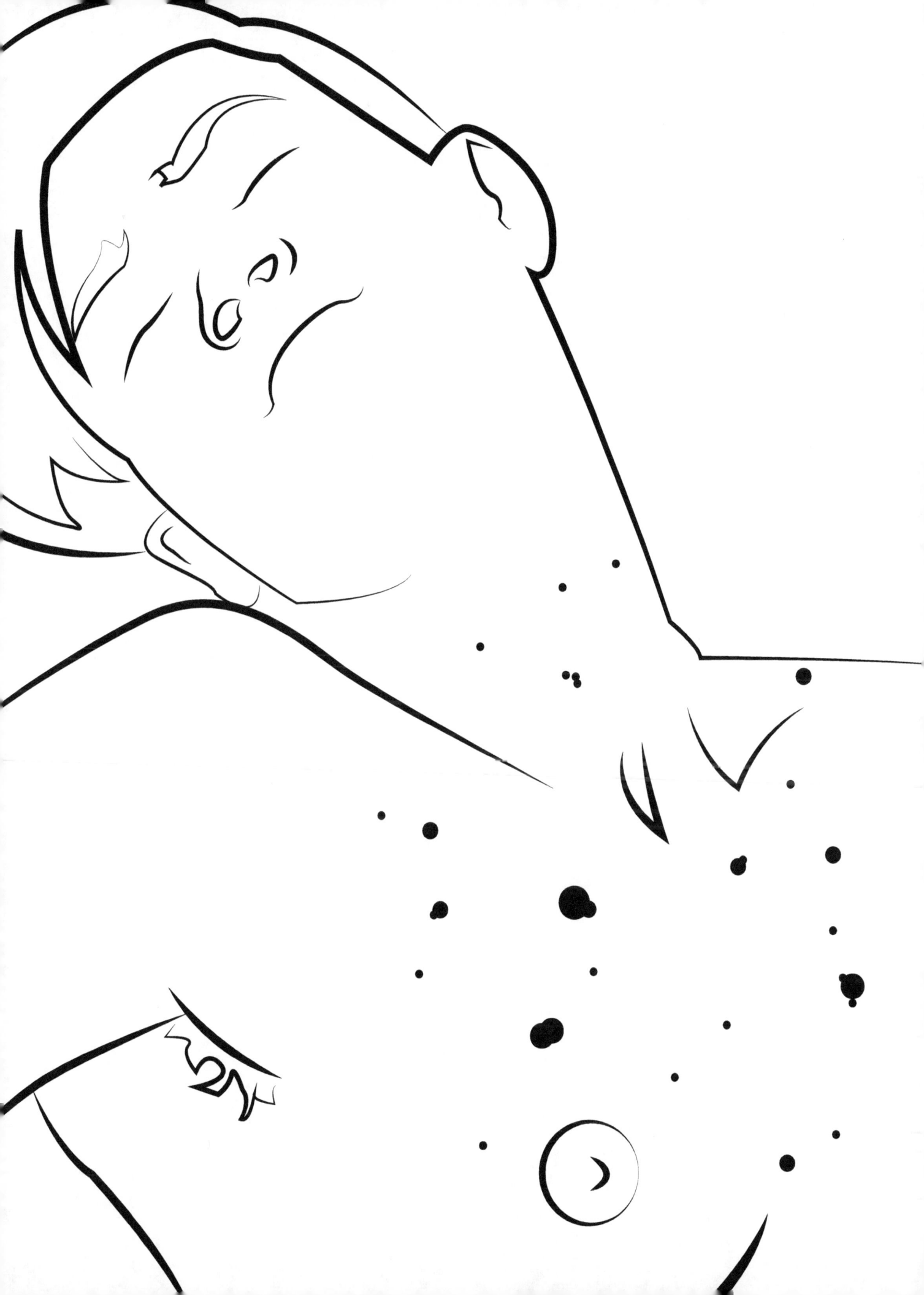

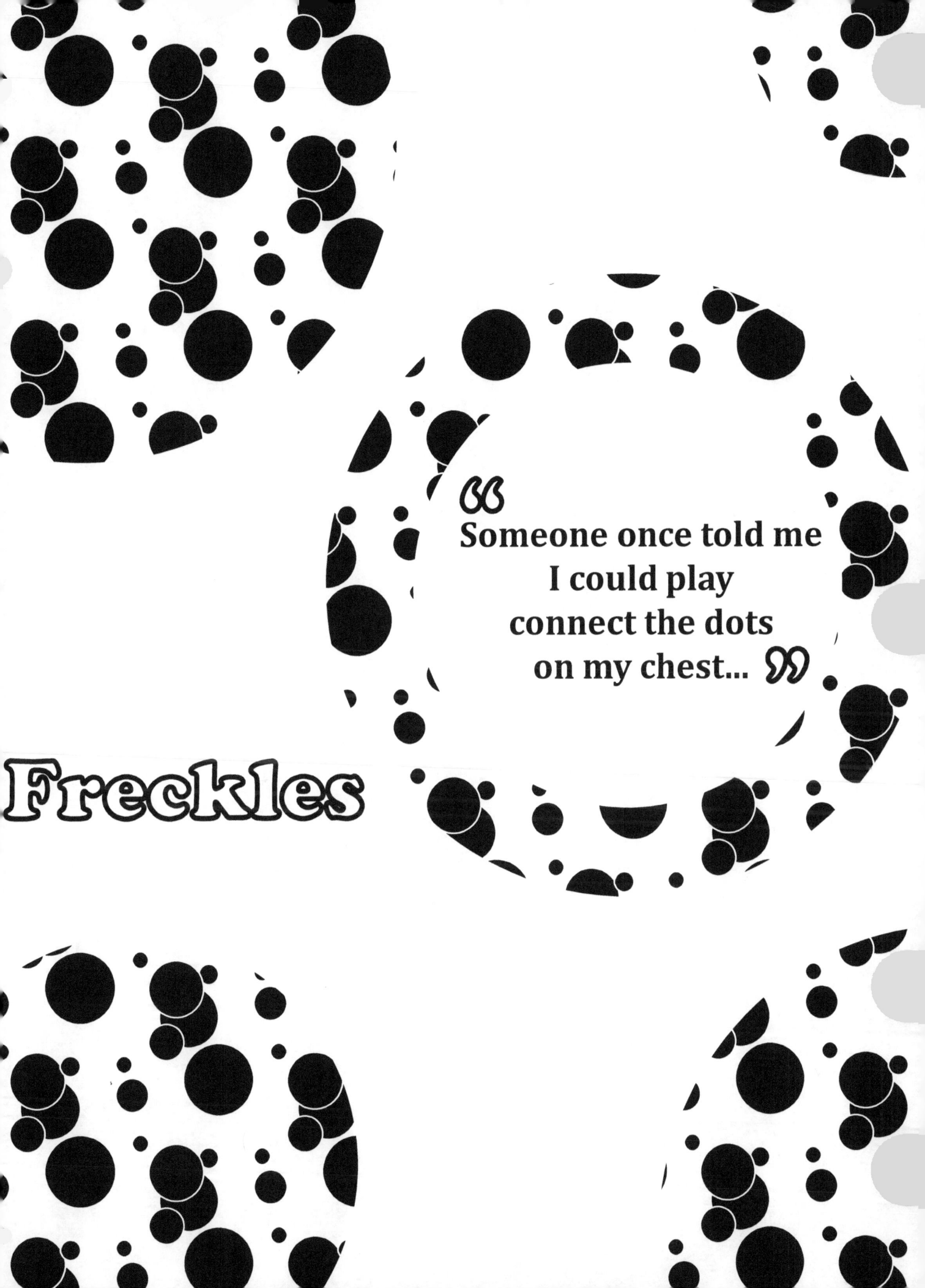

Freckles

" Someone once told me
I could play
connect the dots
on my chest... "

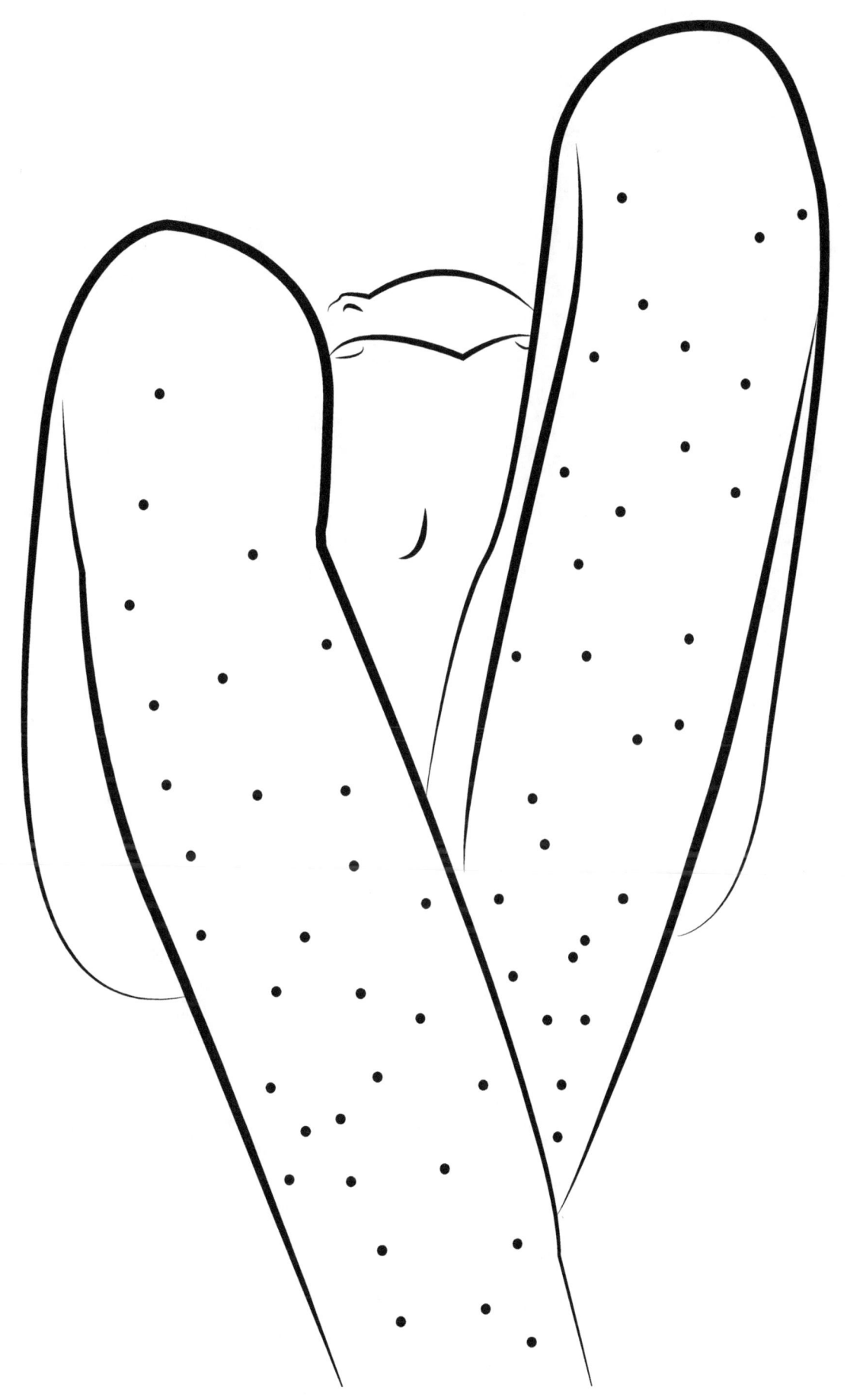

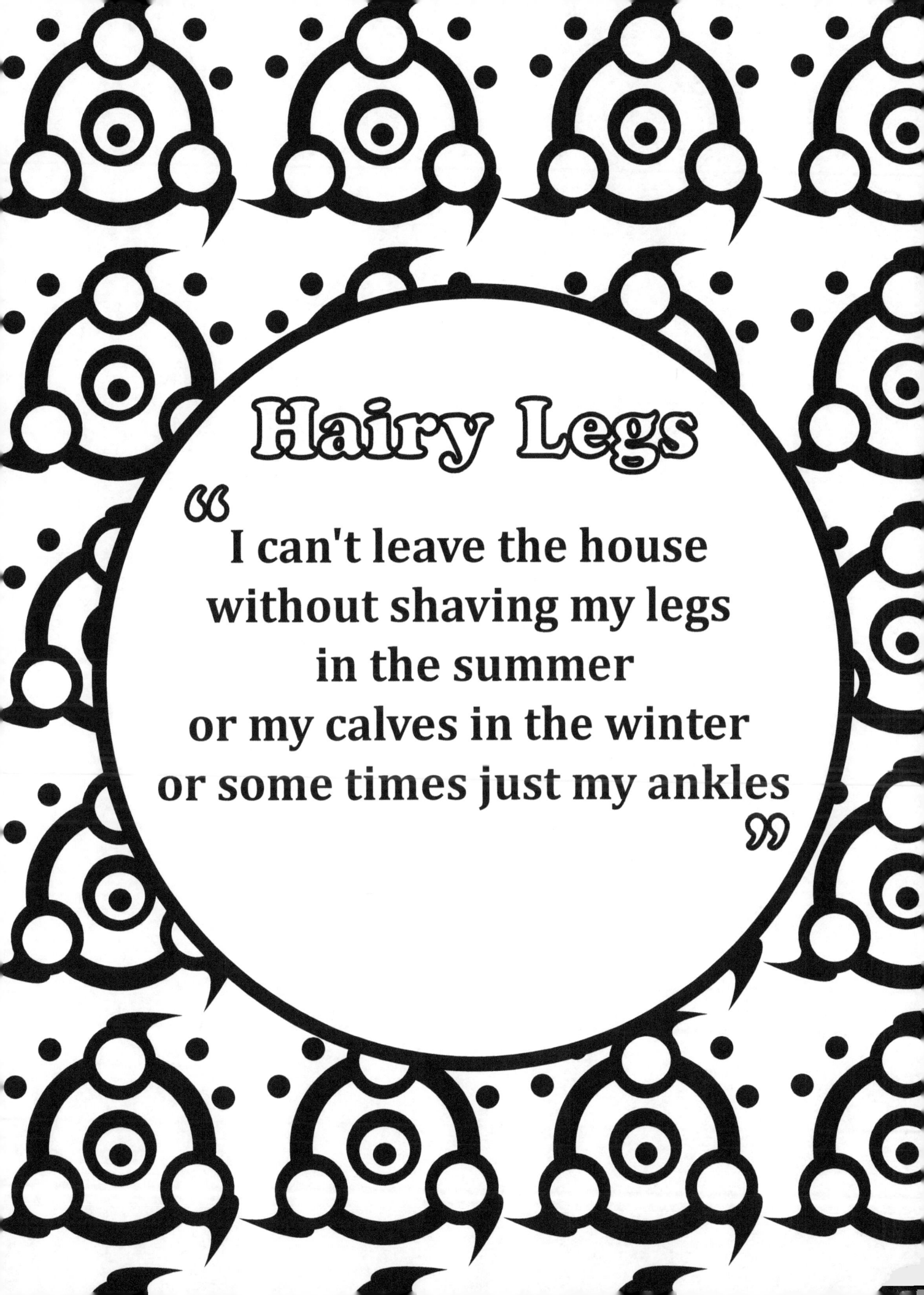

Hairy Legs

"
I can't leave the house
without shaving my legs
in the summer
or my calves in the winter
or some times just my ankles
"

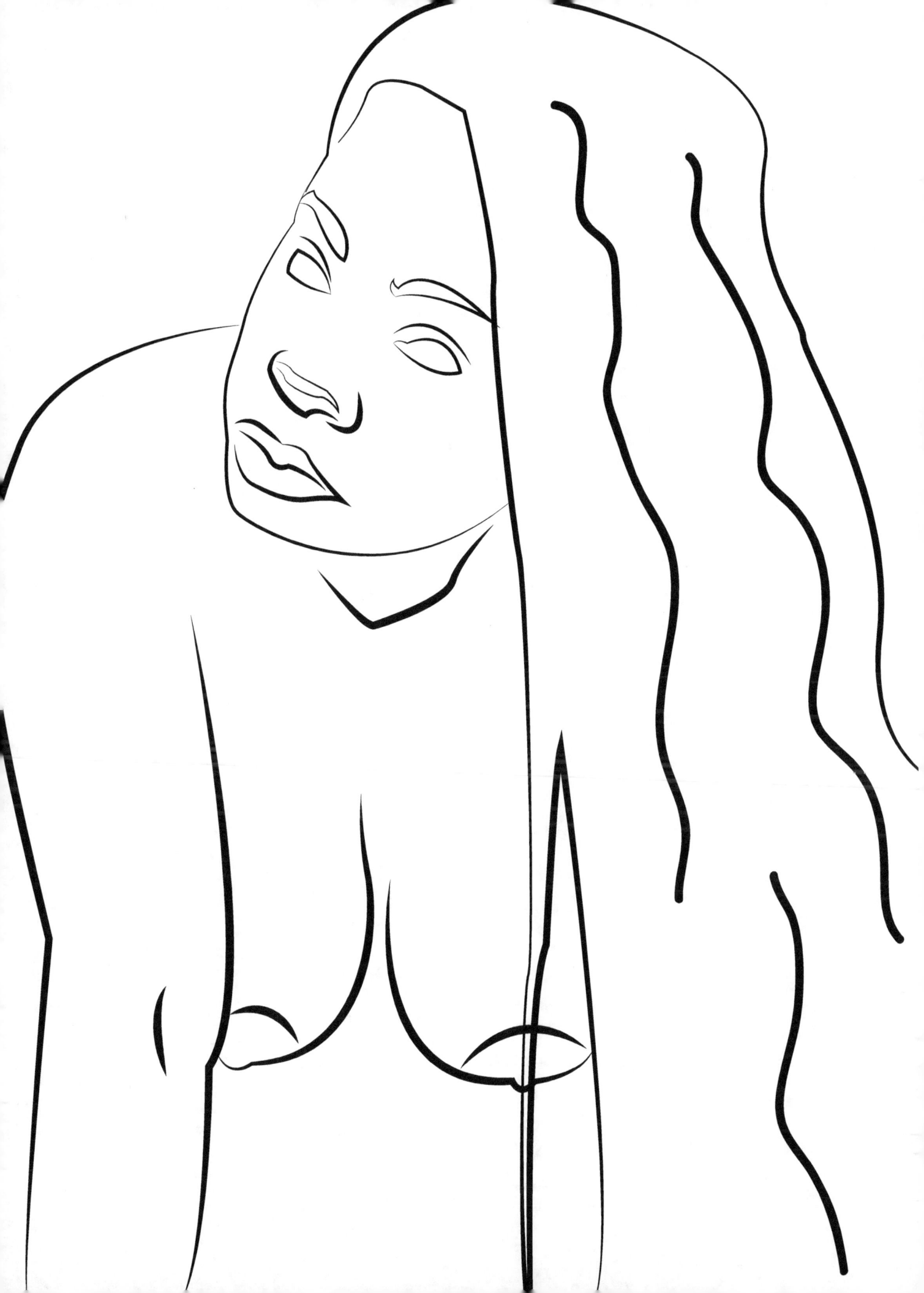

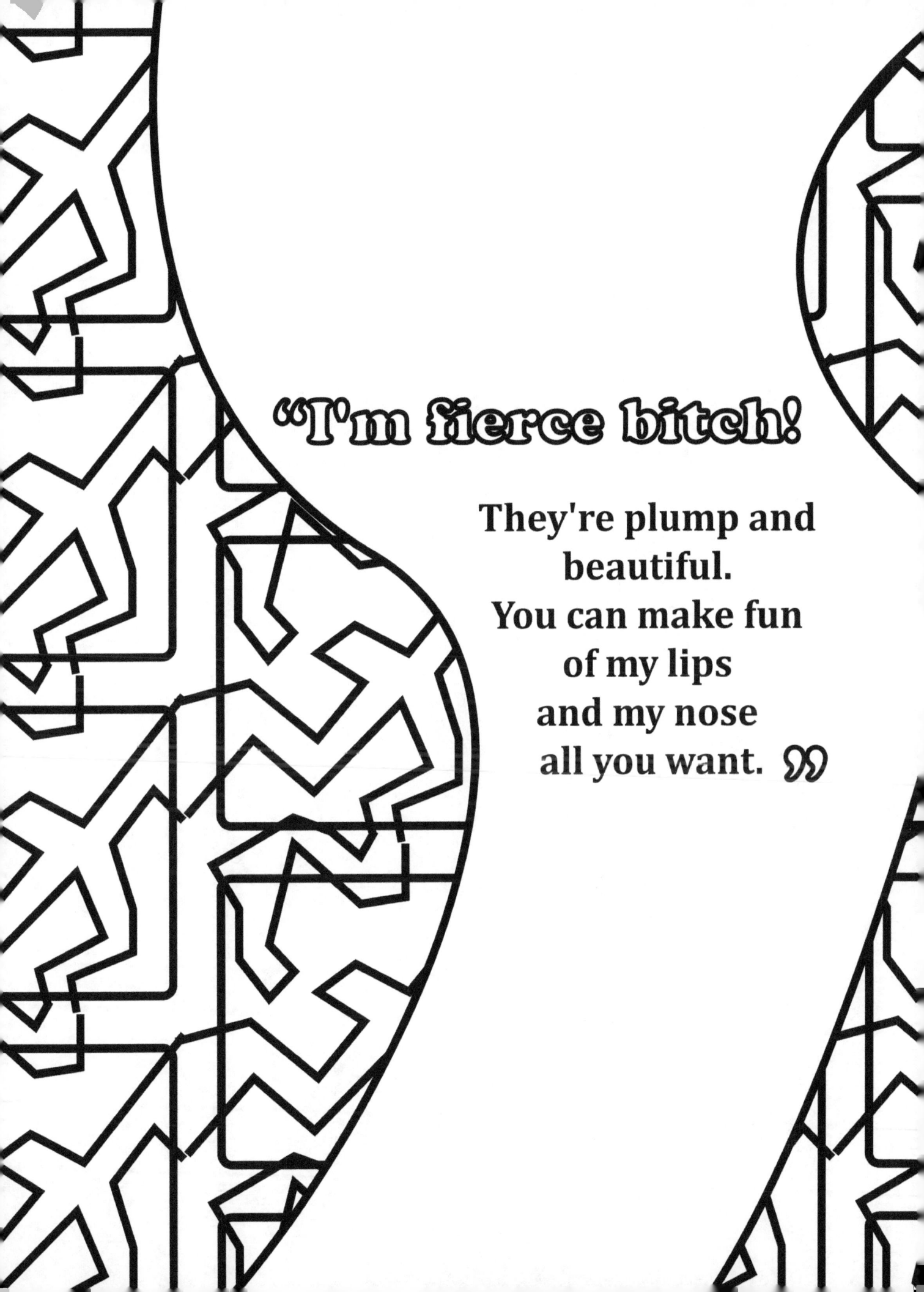

"I'm fierce bitch!

They're plump and
beautiful.
You can make fun
of my lips
and my nose
all you want. "

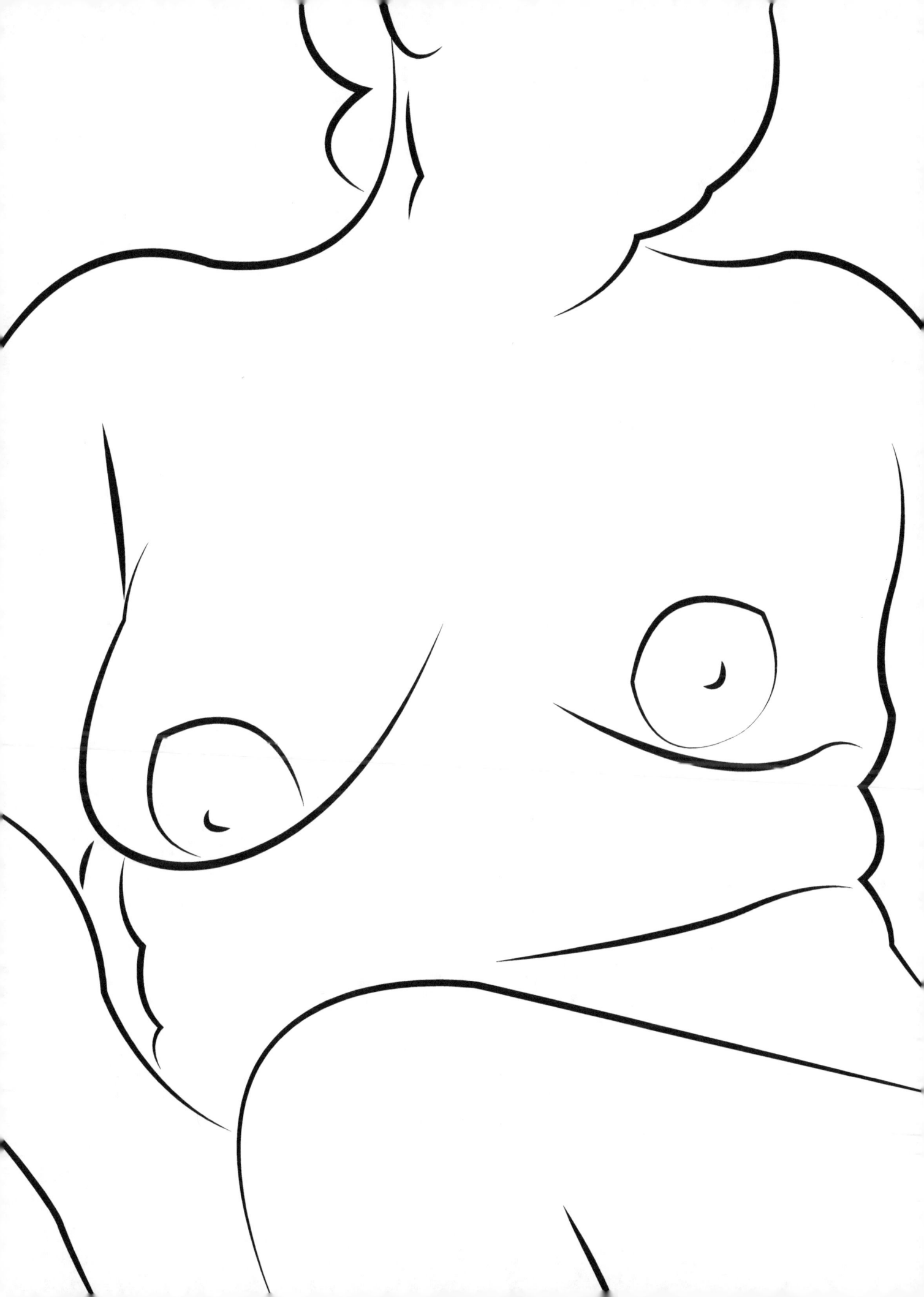

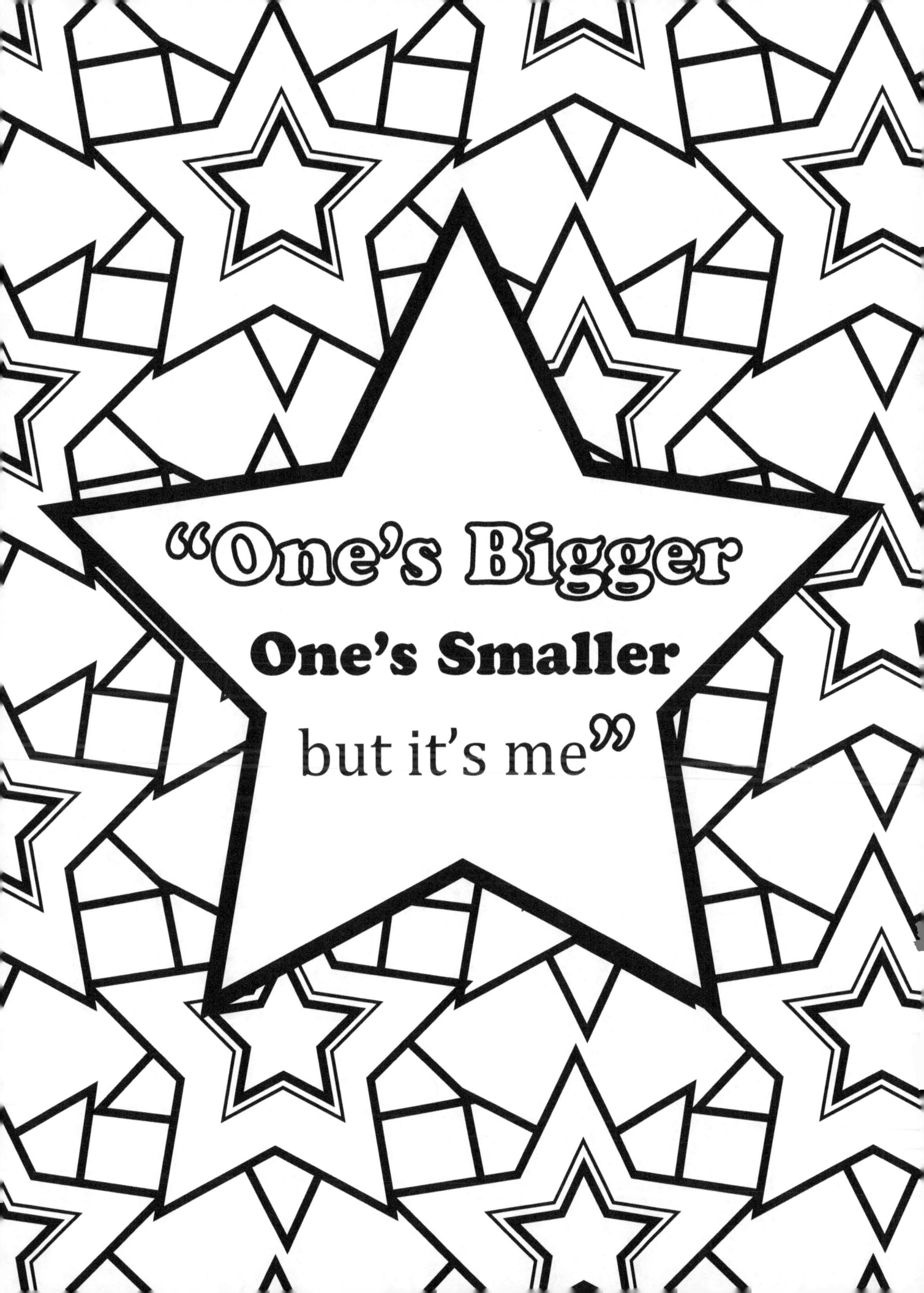

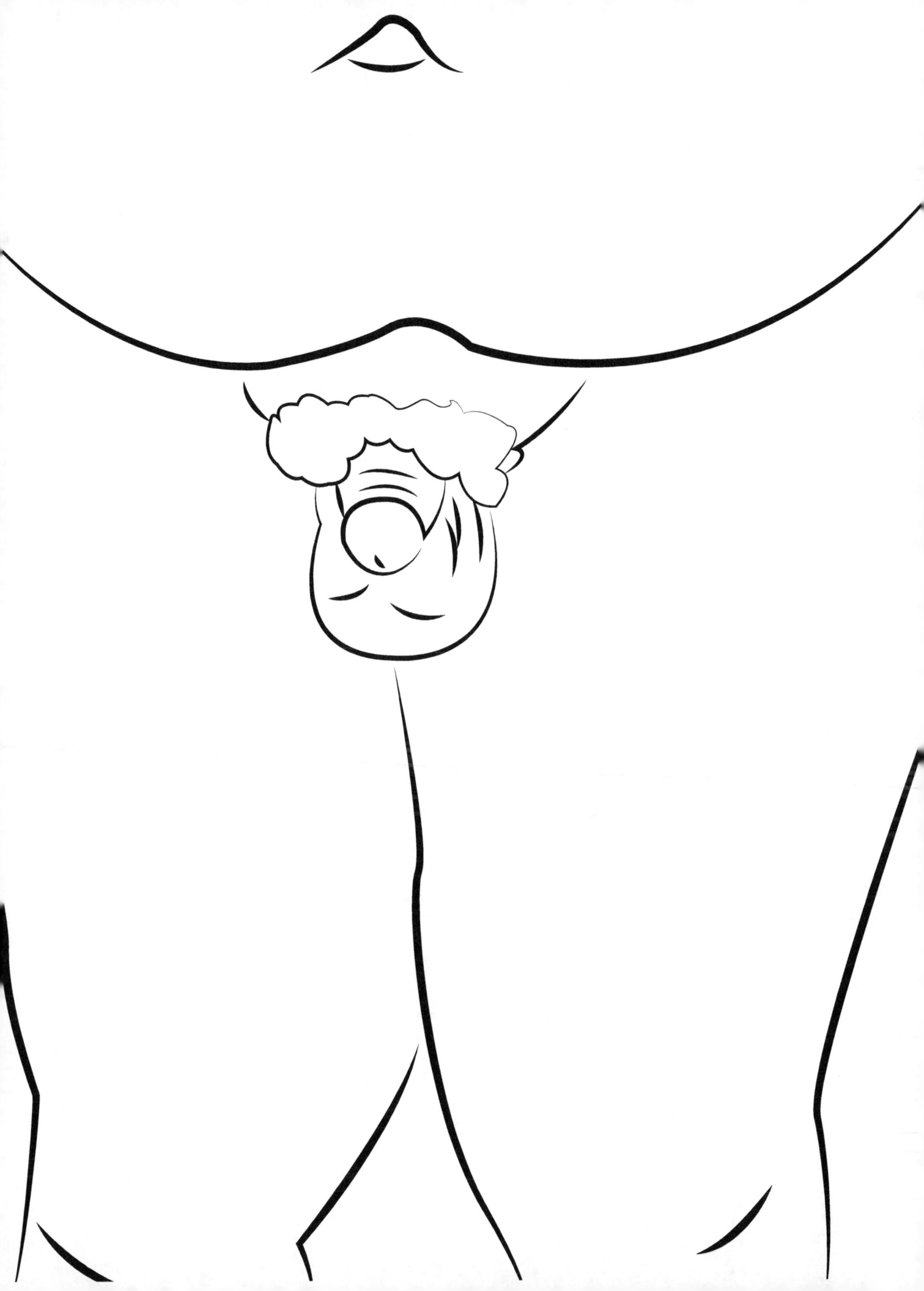

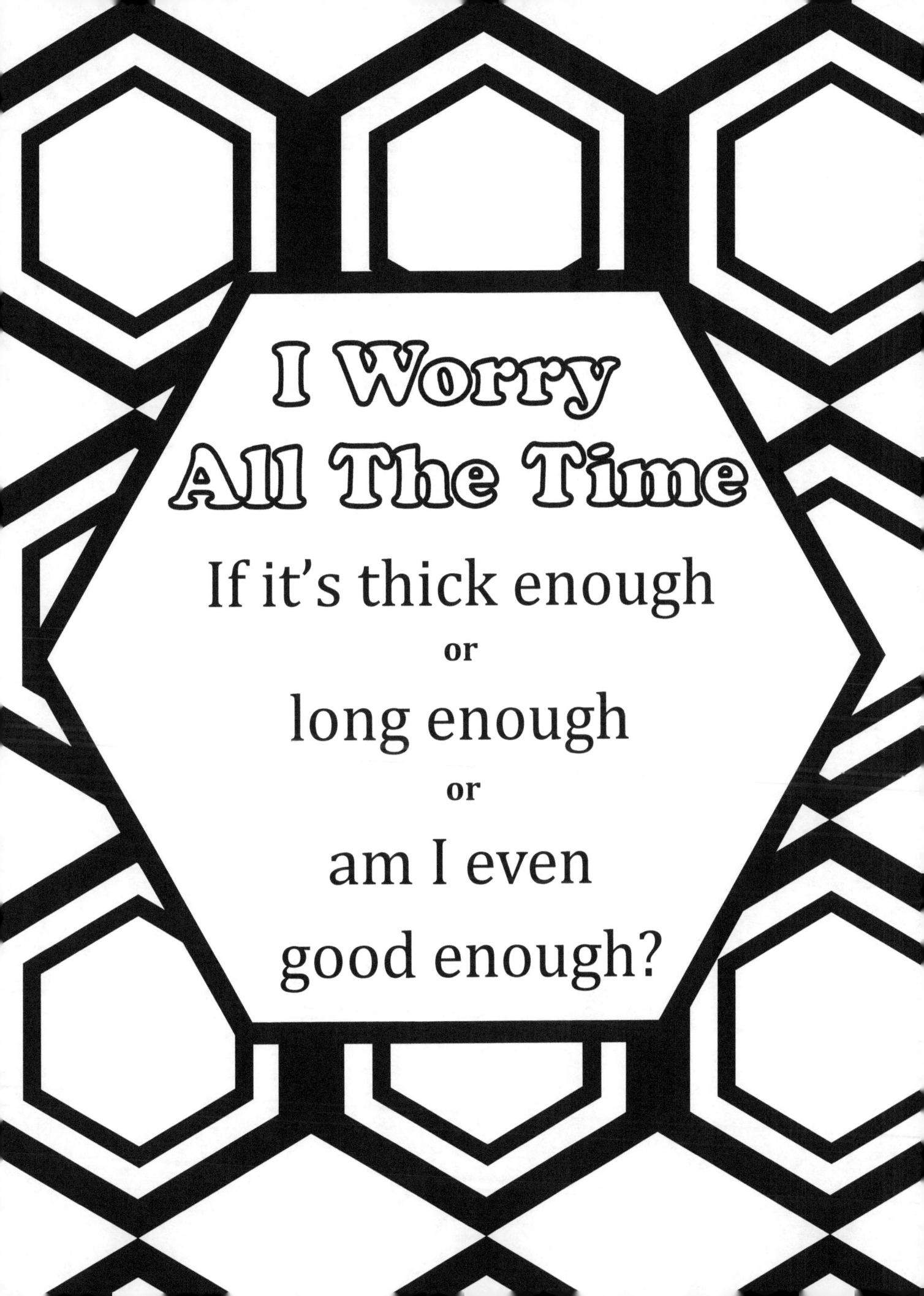

I Worry All The Time

If it's thick enough

or

long enough

or

am I even

good enough?

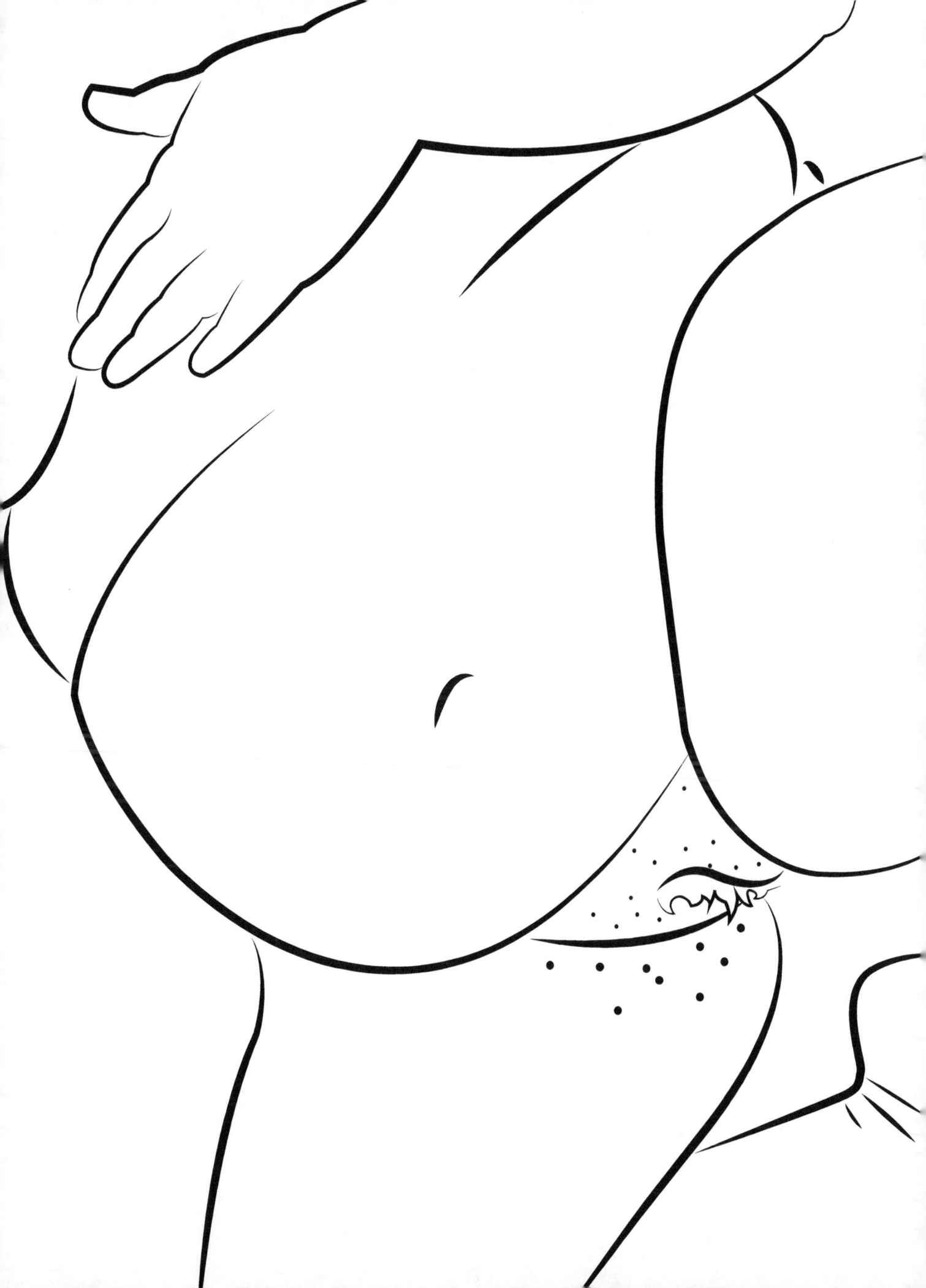

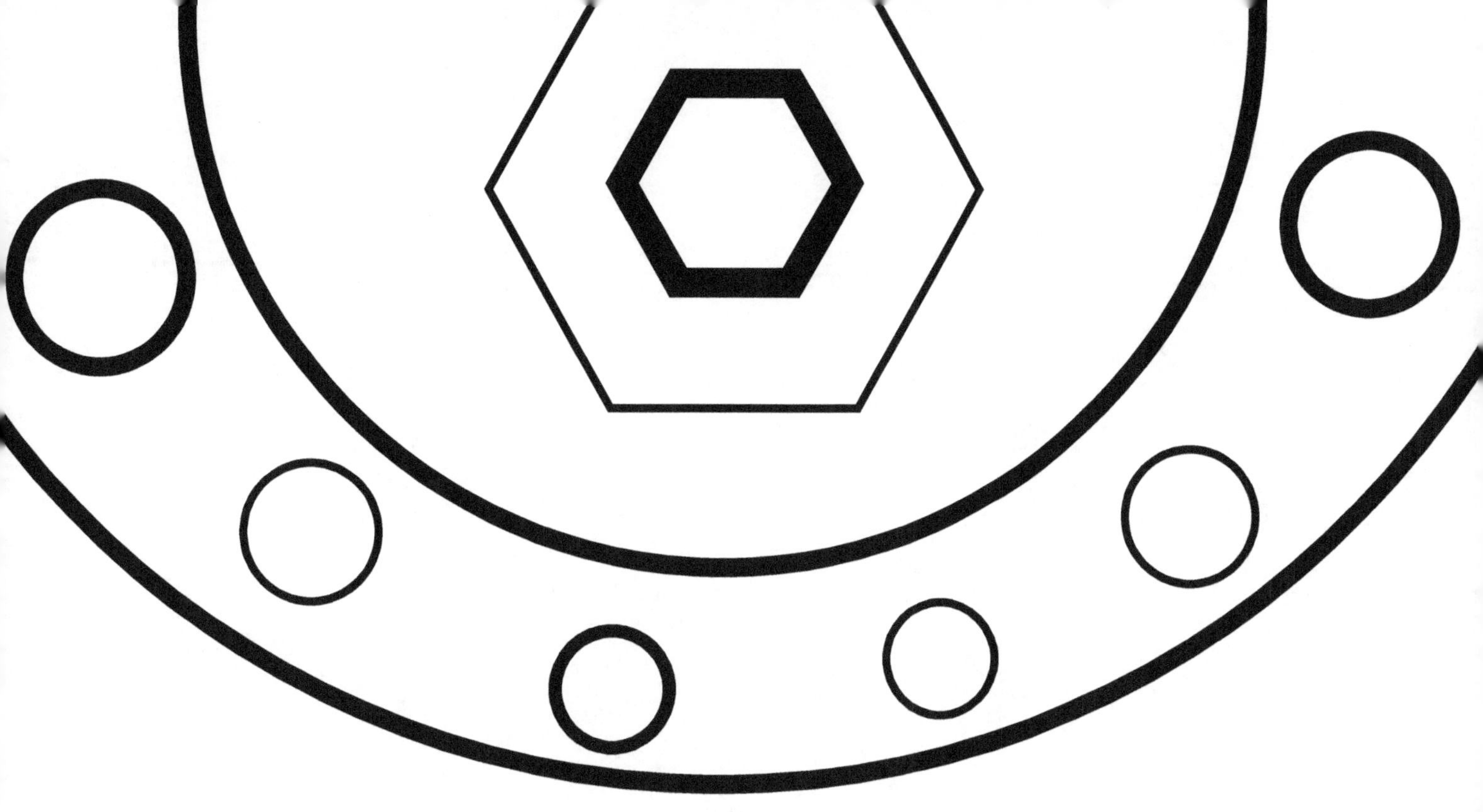

" Hair or not

I once felt it was an issue
but I found someone who will
eat it anyways. "

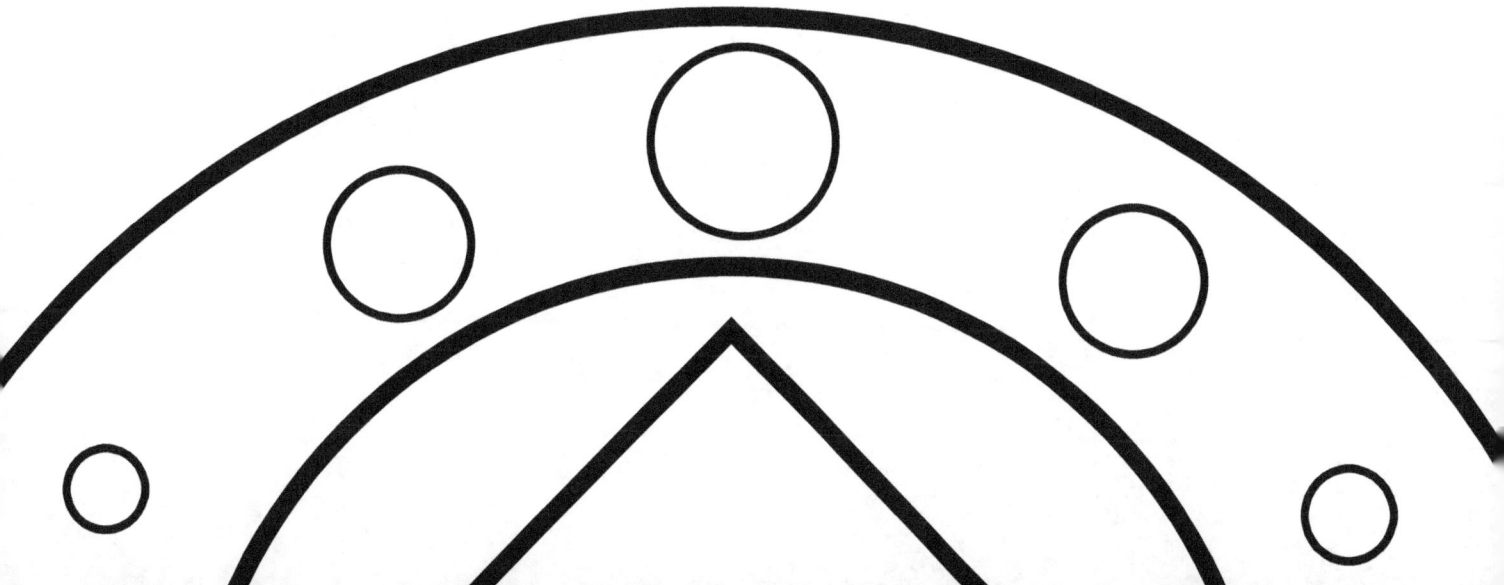